W9-BQU-088

Buzz, Ruby, and Their City Chicks

A True Red-Tailed Hawk Story

Wendy Drexler and Joan Fleiss Kaplan

Photographs by John Harrison, Andy Provost, Ernie Sarro, and John Beattie

(Photographs edited and enhanced by Steve Gladstone)

With immense gratitude to four talented nature photographers who have graciously contributed their photographs and have shared many details of Buzz and Ruby's story: Andy Provost, Ernie Sarro, John Beattie, and especially John Harrison, who worked tirelessly to coordinate the photo pipeline and ensure that we had the best-quality images. We are indebted to renowned hawk authority Paul M. Roberts for reviewing our story for accuracy and for providing an extensive update on Buzz, Ruby, and Belle, a summary of which appears on p. 32. Heartfelt thanks to Dalia Geffen and Julia Price Baron for their many substantive editorial suggestions; to Miriam Maracek, who encouraged us early on; and to Steve Gladstone for obtaining the final high-density photo files, converting them to drawings, and producing the pages of this book.

Photos on pages 1, 2, 4, 7, 8, 9, 10, 11, 12, 13, 14, 17, 18, 19, 26, 28, 29, and back cover by John Harrison. Photos on pages 3, 5, 6, 16, 20, 21, 22, 23, 24, 25, and 27 by Ernie Sarro. Cover photo and photo on page 15 by Andy Provost. Photo on p. 24 by John Beattie.

Copyright © 2016 Wendy Drexler and Joan Fleiss Kaplan

All rights reserved.

ISBN: 0996374744
ISBN-13: 978-0996374743

Buzz and Ruby's wide nest sits high on top of the fourth-floor ledge of an office building. They fly back and forth to their three-foot-wide nest, carrying twigs, bark strips, fresh leaves, and pine needles.

But these are not your average city birds. They have beautiful red tails and brown and white bodies. In fact, Buzz and Ruby are red-tailed hawks. Most red-tails build their nests in trees, but this couple has decided to settle in the city.

Nesting Time

In mid-March, something wonderful happens! Ruby begins to sit on the nest all day and night. What could she be doing? She's keeping three small brown-and-white speckled eggs warm.

Female red-tailed hawks are bigger than the males. This surely helps Ruby, the mom, keep the eggs warm! Ruby does most of the sitting, but Buzz, the dad, also helps. It takes a month for the eggs to hatch. That's a lot of sitting!

Up there on the ledge, their eggs are safe from raccoons, porcupines, and weasels that might eat them. Down below, huge crowds of people are watching them.

Here They Come

In April the first chick pecks through her shell using her sharp egg tooth. Once she breaks out, she no longer needs this tooth and it falls out. Lucy is fluffy and white and mighty big for a newborn chick!

A day later the second chick pecks his way out of his egg. Larry looks just like Lucy.

Where's the Third Chick?

Then at least a week passes. Will there be a third chick?

At long last, Lucky breaks out of his egg. He is much smaller than Lucy and Larry. He will *have* to be lucky to get enough food!

What Will the Chicks Eat?

Buzz is a great hunter. From far away he brings Ruby a pigeon, a squirrel, and a snake with its head bitten off so that she can feed the chicks. How often do you think Buzz returns to the nest with food?

Up to twelve times a day! That's a lot of meals and a lot of flying!

With all the hunting that Buzz has to do, it helps that he has such great eyesight. He can spot his prey from hundreds of feet away! And he's fast! With his four-foot wingspan, Buzz can glide between updrafts of air at speeds up to 60 miles an hour. And when he dives down to catch his prey, he can reach speeds approaching 100 miles an hour! It's a good thing, too, because the chicks are always hungry and screeching for food.

Ruby, with her razor-sharp beak, tears the food into small bites for the chicks. Lucy and Larry gobble the bites down. They push little Lucky to the back of the nest. But Ruby, a very good mother, always saves some food for him.

Ruby Protects Her Chicks

By early May, the chicks have gotten bigger. Ruby can now leave them on their own for a little while.

But one day while Ruby is away, the sky suddenly grows dark. There is thunder and lightning. Rain pelts down. In a flash, Ruby returns to the nest. She opens and spreads her wings wide over her chicks to keep them dry.

On very hot days, Ruby spreads her wings like a beach umbrella, shading her chicks from the sun.

Danger!

The chicks are getting so big that they crowd the nest. Their wing feathers are growing and they are getting ready to fly. Jumping up and down, the fledglings flutter their wings, helicoptering in the wind to make them strong.

But it is dangerous up there for a first flight! What if one of them flies off into a strong wind and can't find a place to land?

Especially for a city bird, this is a most frightening time. Without tree branches for landing, city red-tails must take an all-or-nothing flight. The chicks have only a fifty-percent chance of survival. But if they make it, they can live a long time—some more than 20 years!

Getting Ready to Fledge

It's the middle of May. Lucy, Larry, and Lucky should have fledged days ago! The chicks need courage to take their first, scary flight. What will happen now?

Buzz and Ruby spend hours gliding back and forth with their wings spread wide to show them how.

Ruby flies off and returns, hovering above the nest with a squirrel in her beak. The chicks look up. What is Ruby doing? She drops it on the roof above the nest. The squirrel's tail dangles over the edge to tempt the chicks.

Will they fly up and eat the squirrel?

They don't budge. Not Lucy. Not Larry. Not Lucky. Ruby is fed up! After half an hour, she drops the squirrel into the nest and flies away.

Larry Takes a Leap

But one exciting day at the end of May, Larry hops up and down on the edge of the ledge. Finally feeling brave, he jumps to the roof.

Will Larry be the first to fly away from the nest?

Then . . . pouf! Larry is gone. Fly, Larry, fly!! The first brave red-tailed chick to fly lands proudly on the railing of a nearby roof. He made it!

Watch Out!

But Larry doesn't see the wall of the office building to his side. He takes a hard right turn and crashes into the wall! Did he think the wall was the sky?

Larry falls to the ground and stumbles into the busy road. Oh, no! Buzz and Ruby perch, helplessly watching Larry.

Cars zoom over the hill, heading right toward the frightened fledgling! A woman rushes into the street to stop the traffic. Larry looks right up at her.

It's Not Over Yet

The woman and her friend follow him with a blanket, hoping to guide him to safety. But Larry scurries ahead of them into the parking lot.

Larry tries to hop onto a van but can't reach the roof. He jumps onto a small car. Then he flies to a low roof and up onto a telephone wire.

Larry's First Night Alone

But Larry's adventure isn't over yet. That night, he perches on a pole and it begins to rain. Poor Larry! His wings are too wet for him to fly. He is soaked and exhausted! What a first night to have to spend alone, away from the nest.

Who Will Fledge Next?

Back in the nest, Lucky has been getting ready to fly. A few days after Larry's first flight, Lucky is helicoptering above the nest when a sudden gust of wind catches him by surprise and sweeps him away.

But Lucky, true to his name, is *lucky!* He twists and turns in the air and lands safely on the roof above the nest.

That afternoon there's another storm. Now Lucky's wings are so wet, *he* can't fly. Every time he tries, he flops back to the ground. Lucky jumps onto a car and slips and slides on the wet windshield.

Hours later, in the dark, Lucky flies to safety in a tree. His outer feathers are still wet, but he preens his coat with oils to keep his inside feathers fluffy, dry, and warm.

What about Lucy?

By the crack of dawn the next day, the nest is empty. Lucy, the oldest and largest chick, is gone! She's fledged a week after Larry, and a day after Lucky. (Larger females usually do take more time to fledge than males.)

No one saw her go. But there she is, perched on a truck. All three birds have safely made their first dangerous flight.

But how will the young red-tails learn to feed themselves?

Teaching the Fledglings to Hunt

All hawks are born with the instinct to hunt. Ruby triggers this instinct in her fledglings by grasping a pinecone in her talons and flying over them. She drops it to the ground, pouncing on it. The young hawks begin capturing pinecones and sticks. Soon they will hunt earthworms, insects, and then larger prey, such as squirrels. Buzz and Ruby will gradually stop feeding them, and Lucy, Larry, and Lucky will begin hunting and living on their own.

What about the Empty Nest?

During the summer and fall, the nest sits empty. Lucy, Larry, and Lucky are on their own now. Will Buzz and Ruby come back to use the nest again next year?

When a hawk pair has been able to nest and raise chicks, they tend to stay together. Once or twice a month, Buzz and Ruby return to the nest, freshening it with new twigs to show other red-tailed hawks that this territory still belongs to them. In December, they begin to rebuild the nest to use again.

In mid-March, something wonderful happens! Ruby begins to sit on the nest. A new brood of chicks is on the way.

Buzz and Ruby: An Update

This update is based on an account provided by Paul M. Roberts, a Boston-based hawk expert and director of the Hawk Migration Association of North America.

Buzz, Ruby, and Their Three City Chicks describes events that took place in 2010 on the fourth-floor ledge of an office building in Cambridge, Massachusetts. In 2011, Buzz and Ruby fledged three more chicks from this site. In 2012, Buzz and Ruby were chased from the ledge by peregrine falcons. Making a new nest nearby, the hawks raised two broods, in 2012 and 2013.

Ruby laid her eggs in 2014, but sadly died from eating poisoned rats before the eggs could hatch. Frantic after Ruby's death, Buzz built a new nest on the office-building ledge. Buzz soon bonded with Belle, an adult female without a mate. But Belle showed no interest in this nest.

In 2015, Buzz built another nest, but Belle did not like this nest, either. She flew a mile away, to a quieter residential neighborhood, laying eggs in a nest she may have used before. Only one chick fledged from this nest.

As of 2016, Buzz and Bell are together, successfully raising two chicks, but they face threats from local construction and other red-tailed hawks interested in their territory.

For Paul M. Roberts' extensive posts and updates about Buzz, Ruby, and Belle:
groups.yahoo.com/group/185redtails
For hundreds of his annotated photos of Buzz and Ruby:
www.flickr.com/photos/30136859@N06/sets

What's the Buzz?

Questions to Discuss

1. Have you seen nesting birds? Where were their nests?

2. Have you seen any nests on office buildings?
   - In what ways is a city nest, high on a ledge, a safe place for young chicks?
   - In what ways is it dangerous?

3. What did Buzz and Ruby use to build their nest? (twigs, bark strips, fresh leaves, and pine needles)

4. Do you think Buzz and Ruby are good parents? Why or why not?

5. What did Buzz and Ruby do to make sure their chicks learned the skills they needed to survive?

6. Do you think the chicks were good learners? Why or why not?

7. The chicks had to be very brave to take their first flight from the safety of their nest. When have you been brave?

8. Remember the woman in the story who tried to help Larry get out of the road? Do you think Larry knew she was trying to help him? Why or why not?

9. How did Larry, Lucky, and Lucy fledge and what problems did each bird have? How were their experiences similar?

10. What things did Buzz and Ruby do for their chicks that are similar to what your parents or caregivers do for you?

11. What things did Buzz and Ruby do that your parents or caregivers do not do?

12. Do you know what materials other animals use to build their homes?
    - Beavers use trees, sticks, and mud to build dams in ponds.
    - Termites use wood and saliva to build underground nests.
    - Wasps chew wood and plant fiber into soft pulp. When the pulp dries, it hardens like paper.
    - Foxes dig (burrow) down into the dirt or into the side of a hill or cliff to make their dens.

13. Lucy, Larry, and Lucky hatched from eggs. Do you know any other animals that hatch from eggs?

- Crocodiles, frogs, fish, turkeys, emus
- Peacocks, insects, platypuses, turtles, snakes

14. Bird eggs can be eaten by raccoons, porcupines, snakes, and crows. What other creatures are eaten by larger animals?

- Worms and caterpillars are eaten by birds; insects are eaten by frogs.
- Smaller fish are eaten by larger fish; and small and large fish are eaten by large birds.

Find Out More on Your Own

1. Red-tailed hawks can reach speeds approaching 100 miles an hour. How fast can *you* run? Research the speeds of other animals.

2. A grown red-tailed hawk has a four-foot-wide wingspan. When you stretch your arms straight out to your sides, what is the distance? Find out how the wingspans of other birds compare.

3. The average lifespan for a red-tailed hawk is three to four years at best. Only one in two nestlings survive their first year. If a red-tailed hawk lives to be two, he or she is likely to live four to five years longer. To date, the oldest red-tailed hawk is known to have lived for 28 years. Find out how long other animals can live.

4. Learn about how other animals care for their young. How do their behaviors compare with those of Buzz and Ruby's?

35374975R00021

Made in the USA
Middletown, DE
30 September 2016